Table of Contents

INTRODUCTION 5

CHAPTER ONE 6

What is Aeroponics 6

Why Do You Want An Aeroponic System? 8

Which Aeroponics are you talking about? High or Low 10

High Pressure Aeroponics is True 11

plant-spray1 12

Low Pressure Aeroponics is Cheaper....................... 13

Aerogarden is a Fake 15

Tower Garden aeroponic growing system is NOT TRUE 15

A Deep Look At Aeroponics................................... 17

How Does Aeroponics Work?................................. 19

The Advantages of Aeroponics............................... 22

Equipment Considerations.................................... 24

Different Types of Aeroponics Systems 26

Low Pressure Aeroponics (LPA) Systems 26

High Pressure Aeroponics Systems (HPA)................. 29

Ultrasonic fogger Aeroponics / Fogponics 32

WHICH PLANTS TO GROW?................................... 34

TOOLS NEEDED 36

The Reservoir 39

Water/Nutrient Pump 39

Repeat Cycle Timer...................................... 40

Misting Nozzles 41

Net Cups / Grow Chambers 41

pH Level Consistency with Aeroponics Systems 43

Soil Test...................................... 44

Monitoring EC levels in Your Reservoir.................... 47

Aeroponics Troubleshooting 51

Pump malfunctions...................................... 51

Blocked nozzles 52

Multiple Problems with bacteria and fungi – The One Solution Fix...................................... 53

Maintaining Your Aeroponic System 56

Cleaning 56

The Pros and Cons of Aeroponics 60

In Closing...................................... 62

The History of Aeroponics...................................... 64

Aeroponic History - the beginning...................... 65

Aeroponic System Advancements...................... 66

Some of the key benefits of aeroponics: 68

CHAPTER TWO 73

Vertical Farming 73

Hydroponics 75

Aeroponics 75

Aquaponics.. 76

Rationale for Vertical Farms.................................... 77

What is meant by vertical farming? 87

Expected benefits of vertical farming..................... 89

Year-round crop production in a protected,
managed environment: 89

Advantages of Vertical Farming 92

No-cost restoration of ecosystems: the principle of
"benign neglect" 93

Waste management and urban sustainability ... 100

Social benefits of vertical farming 105

CHAPTER THREE 109

Aeroponic towers: 109

AirGrown Aeroponics Growing Tower............... 116

Thirty plant sites 116

Vertical growing system....................................... 117

The inventor 117

Mother helped me... 117

The business 118

Followed NASA in aeroponics............................ 118

Vegatables cleaner, tastier................................. 119

CONCLUSION 120

INTRODUCTION

The Aeroponic Tower system is not only described as user-friendly, but also believed to be the most efficient, "because you start with germination and will not need to touch the plant again until harvest time." It is also efficient in terms of irrigation, as "each section has its own water, and depending on the system, you can control the pH, temperature and nutrients."

The system uses 97% of all the water and nutrients and just 3% is evaporated. Because it is a closed loop system, it recirculates everything. Also, as a result of the water temperature being regulated, the towers, which are installed within the greenhouse, act as radiators, and the temperature outside the ring is about 10 degrees different than inside, which ensures perfect growing conditions.

CHAPTER ONE
What is Aeroponics

So let's get to the true root meaning of what aeroponics is. The word Aeroponics is derived from two Latin words meaning aero (air) and ponic (work), air at work. In other words, the whole plant, roots and all, are suspended in mid air. Simple put the roots are not covered, not buried, not submerged in any form of liquid or matter, they are revealed openly in thin air.

It's so simple and basic. Why do so many complicate the issue? Because, they have their own agenda to make or they want to profit from it. Please, don't be taken by such false advertisement.

Good! We got that out of the way. We will return to the definition later. But for now let's focus on what aeroponics really is.

Getting right to the point, Aeroponics is the fastest way to grow plants than any other growing method. Aeroponics is the process of growing plants in thin air where its roots are exposed to a misty environment. No soil or aggregate medium is used to support the plant.

Aeroponics is an advance method of developing plant growth, flowering, fruiting and health for most plant species and cultivators. Aeroponics is a method of growing plants suspended (hanging) in mid air without the use of soil or any medium. The bare exposed roots get all of their nutrients from the environment it's in. There are two forms of aeroponics: High Pressure Aeroponics (HPA) and Low Pressure Aeroponics (LPA).

Carbon dioxide in the air is necessary for healthy plant growth. However, oxygen is needed for roots to absorb the nutrients that surround them. True aeroponics is conducted in air enriched with micro-droplets of nutrient water.

Why Do You Want An Aeroponic System?

One of the major advantages aeroponic systems have over other types of growing methods is the lack of disease problems.

Because there is no soil there are no soil born diseases and also no soil borne pests. Also because the roots hang in the air these systems are free of the root rot problems that can occur with hydroponic growing systems.

These systems do not use air stones because there is no need for additional aeration. The root environment and falling mist or droplets provide all the aeration that is needed.

Growing media is not used in aeroponics. This saves money on operating costs and eliminates storing and disposing of spent media.

Because you don't need media or noisy air pumps aeroponics is ideal for stealth growing. It is totally silent. Also you need to haul a lot less water and water weight and leaks can be a big issue with a hydroponic system, especially if you are growing in an upstairs apartment or an attic.

Aeroponic plants need 50% less nutes and what you do need to mix is less than any other system. This is another money saver for the grower.

Your plants will mature faster. An aeroponic grow will mature 7 – 10 days ahead of a soil grow. Both aeroponic and hydroponic systems will produce higher yields than a soil or soiless system. It is hard to say if one will out yield the other because systems vary so much, but the aeroponic plants will be superior to those grown any other way.

An aeroponic system grows superior weed simply because healthy plants with healthy root systems produce the best weed. Because you need less fertilizer the need to flush is reduced and the smoke is never harsh. You will also find that smell in the grow room and humidity levels are more controllable too.

So why do you want an aeroponic system? In a nutshell you will grow the best weed possible at lower cost, grow it faster and your plants will be disease free.

Which Aeroponics are you talking about? High or Low

This opens another issue about aeroponics. There are two types or forms of aeroponic systems. The first one is HPA (High Pressure Aeroponics), and the other is LPA (Low Pressure Aeroponics).

HPAs are considered to be True Aeroponics and was used by NASA to grow vegetables. It also is the most expensive and the most complicated growing system to build. However, HPAs use less resources for plant grow: 98% less water, 60%

less fertilizer, and 100% less pesticides (no pesticides), all supported by NASA laboratory studies.

LPAs are lower cost system. LPA systems are the most common used and built by DIYers.

High Pressure Aeroponics is True

The HPA (True Aeroponics) system was revolutionized by NASA in the 1990's by reporting it as the most efficient way to grow plants in space. Studies have shown many benefits of growing plants with aeroponic techniques on both Earth and in space.

plant-spray1

HPA systems must operate at a high pressure, normally above 80 PSI, but ideally at 100 PSI. The high pressure is used to atomize the nutrient water through a small orifice (hole) to create water droplets of 50 microns or less in diameter, in other words a fine mist like hair spray.

One micron is one-millionth of a meter. The average diameter of human hair is 80 microns. So we are talking about a really tiny water drop.

HPA also must run on a much accurate time cycle. HPAs might run 1 to 5 seconds on, and then off for three to five minutes. Specific components are required in controlling the timing interval and creating the proper size mist.

The basic components of a HPA are as follows:

1. High-Pressure water pump

2. Pre-Pressurize Accumulator Tank

3. Electrical-Solenoid hooked to an adjustable relay timer

4. Pressure switch

5. Mister nozzles

Low Pressure Aeroponics is Cheaper

LPA systems use a standard magdrive pump couple to some PVC or tubing, and a few miniature sprinkler heads. The water spray from an LPA sprinkler head has large droplets that drown the plant roots.

LPAs generally run the pump 24 hours and 7 days a week, continually wetting the roots. This works well, and is cheap and easy to build. However they are not as efficient as HPA systems.

Also, for this to be truly an aeroponics system the reservoir must be separated from the grow chamber of the plants.

The basic components of a LPA are as follows:

1. High flow water pump

2. Micro sprinklers

Aeroponic systems on the market

Getting back to the definition of Aeroponics: Air at work – This means the plant roots are suspended in midair.

Simply put the plant roots are not covered, not buried, not submerged in any liquid or matter; they are openly suspended in thin air.

So if some or all of the roots are sitting in any liquid, then it's not aeroponics. Any system using a single container to grow and store nutrients, can't be aeroponics.

Aerogarden is a Fake

Aerogarden is Not aeroponics – Ginger Booth, the Indoor Salad Lady, calls it a glorified nutrient film technique hydroponics system. It's sold on the market alluding it's aeroponics. However, it's just a twisted hydroponic system. The plant roots are submerged in a pool of water. Guess what? It's a single container solution.

Tower Garden aeroponic growing system is NOT TRUE

Tower Garden is aeroponics LPA style, it's not True Aeroponics. The system drips the nutrient over plant roots in a hollow tube. I like Tim Blank the inventor. Due to the Tower Garden being easy to operate and includes a very supportive network, it has become popular with many gardeners. However, it's overly sold as THE AEROPONIC system which it's not. The Tower is sold as part of a multi-level-marketing company that became successful providing and healthy choices. Remember, true aeroponics must atomize the nutrient to a fine mist using high pressure.

A Deep Look At Aeroponics

As our soil quality begins to deteriorate, many people are looking for alternative methods to grow fresh vegetables for their future homes. Because of this reason, hydroponics agriculture will become more popular in the future.

Aeroponics is a simple concept yet it is the most technical among all 6 types of hydroponic systems. Aeroponic system is used by a lot of home growers because it has brought really good results for them.

Aeroponics is actually a subset of the hydroponic system. However, with the hydroponics method, plants use water as the growing medium while aeroponics uses no growing medium at all. This technique was invented during the 1940s and since then, many researchers have added to the theory and application of this method. Aeroponics is considered one of the best methods to grow plants in a soil-free environment and the need for this method has been growing due to a clear need for a more convenient way to grow plants.

In the aeroponic system, plants are not contained in any solid material such as Rockwool or soil. Instead, plant roots are hung in the air in a grow chamber in a closed-loop system. The roots are sprayed with nutrient-rich water or fine, high-pressure mist containing nutrient-rich solutions at certain intervals.

This makes aeroponics a more advanced form than the hydroponic wicking systems, deep water culture, and other types

How Does Aeroponics Work?

Vegetables out of thin air? Learn more about this environmentally-friendly approach to food production. Towers and other vertical approaches are increasingly popular for aeroponics systems. Since the roots have need to spread out, this is a clever way to save space. A vertical setup also allows misting devices to be placed at the top, allowing gravity to distribute the moisture.

Aeroponic systems nourish plants with nothing more than nutrient-laden mist. The concept builds off that of hydroponic systems, in which the roots are held in a soilless growing medium, such as coco coir, over which nutrient-laden water is periodically pumped. Aeroponics simply dispenses with the growing medium, leaving the roots to dangle in the air, where they are periodically puffed by specially-designed misting devices.

In aeroponics systems, seeds are "planted" in pieces of foam stuffed into tiny pots, which are exposed to light on one end and nutrient mist on the other. The foam also holds the stem and root mass in place as the plants grow.

Further more, due to no root zone media for plants to anchor in, you need to prepare a support collar that will hold stems in place. These collars must be rigid enough to hold plants upright and keep the roots in place but flexible enough to allow room for roots to grow.

The pump and sprinkler system creates vapor (which is a hydro-atomized spray mixture of water, nutrients and growth hormones) out of the nutrient-rich solution and sprays the mist in the reservoir, engulfing the dangling plant roots and absorbed by them. This spray provides the exact amount of moisture which stimulates the plant's growth and allows it to develop turgidly.

The timer supplies the timed spray intervals and duration for the plants. Some people think that growing plants in aeroponic system would be frailer compared to hydroponics. But that's not true. The secret of aeroponic system all lies in the amount of oxygen exposed to the roots without a root zone media limiting it.

Thanks to this, the plant roots will develop rapidly and grow in a moist air-rich environment. If you want to see their development rate, just lift up the growing chamber to see how they are growing.

The Advantages of Aeroponics

Who knew naked roots could survive, much less thrive? It turns out that eliminating the growing medium is very freeing for a plants' roots: the extra oxygen they are exposed to results in faster growth. Aeroponic systems are also extremely water-efficient. These closed-loop systems use 95 percent less irrigation than plants grown in soil. And since the nutrients are held in the water, they get recycled, too.

In addition to these efficiencies, aeroponics' eco-friendly reputation is bolstered by the ability to grow large quantities of food in small spaces. The approach is mainly employed in indoor vertical farms, which are increasingly common in cities – cutting down on the environmental costs of getting food from field to plate. And because aeroponics systems are fully enclosed, there is no nutrient runoff to foul nearby waterways. Rather than treating pest and disease with harsh chemicals, the growing equipment can simply be sterilized as needed.

Equipment Considerations

All aeroponics systems require an enclosure to hold in the humidity and prevent light from reaching the roots (this is typically a plastic bin with holes drilled for each plant), plus a separate tank to hold the nutrient solution. Beyond these basic components, there are a few other things to consider in devising an aeroponic system to suit your needs.

Some aeroponics systems are designed to be used horizontally, like a traditional planting bed. But towers and other vertical approaches are increasingly popular – since the roots need to spread out, this is a clever way to save space. Vertical systems are also popular because the misting devices may be placed at the top, allowing gravity to distribute the moisture.

Another dichotomy in aeroponic equipment: high-pressure versus low-pressure systems.

Low-pressure systems, which rely on a simple fountain pump to spray water through the misters, are inexpensive and suitable for DIY construction. This approach is sometimes called "soakaponics," as low-pressure misters are capable of producing only a light spray, kind of like a tiny sprinkler, not true mist.

For true mist – meaning moisture floats in the air and more effectively delivers nutrients to the roots – you need higher water pressure than an ordinary pump can provide. Thus, professional aeroponics systems rely on a pressurized water tank capable of holding 60 to 90 psi, along with top-quality misters capable of delivering the finest possible puff of moisture.

Hydroponics suppliers increasingly stock a full-line of aeroponics equipment, from the nutrients, pots, pumps, timers, and tubing you need for a DIY system to fully-automated turnkey aero-farms.

Different Types of Aeroponics Systems

Low Pressure Aeroponics (LPA) Systems

This is the most commonly used aeroponic type used by most hydroponic hobbyists due to its ease to set up, availability at any hydroponic shop, and low cost.

They're also the most widely available in a variety of places, not limited to hydroponic specialist suppliers.

It is possible to make your own LPA system using PVC for the piping, attaching misters to them and using a fountain or pond pump secured to a reservoir.

You don't need a special pump for an LPA system. What you do need is enough pressure to create a mist in the reservoir. Low-pressure creates droplet size much different from the high-pressure aeroponic system.

The problem with finding the right pump for a DIY setup are that pond and fountain pumps don't tend to have a PSI rating. Instead, it's GPH (gallons per hour) and head height.

The head height is more important when choosing a good submersible pump for an LPA system because the higher the head height is, the more pressure is needed to pump the water up 'til it reaches the misters.

You just need to be sure your reservoir is tall enough to accommodate the head height. For best results, each spray should be angled upwards to spray above the roots and have each spray from the nozzles overlap slightly. You want the spray to create a fine mist and then the water to run from the top of the plant roots, then trickle down and drop back into the reservoir.

What you don't want to do is angle the sprinklers to direct the water straight at the roots. That would drench them and likely drown them resulting in what some aeroponic growers term as soakaponics because the roots get soaked rather than misted.

Depending on the size of container you're using, you could have just three sprinklers, or for larger setups, six or more sprinklers attached.

Several things factor into your water pump to get an ideal mist within the reservoir.

The head height because the pressure needs to be forceful enough to travel up the piping to the misters.

The more GPH the pump can push through the system to the head height required, the higher a pressure you'll get.

The number of misters used will affect its efficiency because with each mister, there's going to be a slight drop in pressure.

Always remember that with a low pressure aeroponic system, you need to use the two ratings. GPH and head height.

And remember this part…

Whatever you think you need, go higher because you can always decrease the water pressure but you can never increase it without upgrading to a more powerful pump.

High Pressure Aeroponics Systems (HPA)

This type of Aeroponics is more advanced and quite costly to set up as it would require specialized equipment. So they are often used in the commercial production rather than home growers. This type of setup can really only be described as the commercial farming method of the future.

Using HPA systems is extremely technical and you can just imagine the cost it would be to set up a farm like this, which is why it's only suited to commercial growers needing to grow more per harvest and get more yields per year.

The HPA must run at very high pressure to atomize water into tiny water droplets of 50 microns or less.

This system creates such a fine droplet size that create more oxygen for the root zone than the LPA, making it the most efficient system among all aeroponic types.

A general HPA system pump will start with a range 60 to 90 PSI. The more powerful the pump, the finer the spray. For a professional grade setup, you'd be looking at a pump capable of delivering a steady flow of 100 PSI.

Regulating the frequency is where problems set in because these are running 24/7, so you can expect the pump to need replacing more frequently. And that's just to water up to a half dozen plants. When you get into the hundreds, you're then looking at a far higher cost for misters, pumps and tanks.

To extend the life of an HPA pump, a pressurized accumulator tank is used in a professional HPA system. Using an accumulator tank, there's water and pressurized air used so that the pump doesn't have to work as hard, and to maintain a steady PSI.

Due to the high cost of setting up an HPA system, there's no use for them for home growers. They are suited to urban farming as they are capable of producing far more yields per harvest and more harvests per year.

It's the HPA system that focuses on getting minuscule water droplets of under 50 microns.

Low pressure systems won't produce as small of water droplets, but there will still be a fine mist created by the pump and the sprinkler heads.

Ultrasonic fogger Aeroponics / Fogponics

Ultrasonic fogger Aeroponics, or commonly called fogponics, is another interesting type of Aeroponic system. Fogponics is a more recent advancement in aeroponics that really takes things to another level. Instead of your plant roots being suspended in the air and sprayed with a fine mist, a fogponics system doesn't use a pump; it uses ultrasonic technology.

As the name means, growers would use an ultrasonic fogger to atomize water into super small droplets of water. These are very tiny and you will see it in the form of fog.

It's a disc that's submerged in the water and vibrates at extremely high frequencies that turns the water into a gas form getting water micron sizes down to just one micron and often less.

To really comprehend how small that is, one micron is equal to 1 millionth of a meter. In inches, it's 0.00004."

Though plants roots find it easier to absorb water in tiny size, there's little moisture in the fog created, and when running over time, it can easier create the salt that can clog these foggers than other Aeroponic types.

WHICH PLANTS TO GROW?

You can use this system to grow nearly any type of plants and cultivars such as vegetables, nursery stock, houseplants, and bedding. Hundreds of species of plants have been tested and grown successfully by commercial greenhouse owners, researchers and nursery operate using this technique.

Anything, in theory. In practice, aeroponics systems are primarily used for the same applications as hydroponics systems, including leafy greens, culinary herbs, marijuana, strawberries, tomatoes, and cucumbers. One exception is root crops, which are impractical in a hydroponic system, but well-suited to aeroponics, as the roots have plenty of room to grow and are easily accessible for harvesting.

Other vegetable crops are possible but have more complex nutrient requirements. Fruiting shrubs and trees are impractical in aeroponics systems due to their size.

As all plants need nutrients, the organism will spend a valuable amount of energy growing roots to find these pockets of nutrients in the soil for flower formulation and growth. With hydroponics and aeroponics, nutrients are instead delivered straight to the roots.

Compared to regular hydroponic plants, the plants tend to grow faster and absorb more nutrients because the roots are exposed to more oxygen. Also, there are fewer threats of diseases around root zone disease because there's no place for debris or pathogen to reside.

However, you need to be aware of the fact that aeroponic system chambers are constantly wet with nutrients spray which is convenient for harmful bacteria and fungi to develop. Therefore, it is important to clean and sterilize these misters before using, and occasionally take out and keep these chambers treated with the hydrogen peroxide solution, which can be purchased at any quality hydroponic store.

TOOLS NEEDED

What you will need:

A reservoir/container to hold the nutrient solution

Nutrient pump

Mist nozzles

Tubing to distribute water from the nutrient pump to the mister heads in the growing chamber

Baskets to suspend plants

Enclosed growing chamber for the root zone

Watertight containers for the growing chamber where the plant's root systems will be

Timer (preferable a cycle timer) to turn on and off the pump

You can purchase these tools at the local gardening/hydroponic supply store or online.

It's quite easy to understand how an aeroponic system works. The purpose of the plant roots hanging in mid-air is to get them exposed to oxygen as much as possible. The high volume of oxygen exposure will stimulate their growth and help them grow faster than they would in the soil, which is a very important benefit of this type of system. This can be seen in the massive root growth of the plants. It has also been proven that this technique increase crop yield X10 compared to using soil. Not only will you be able to collect healthier plants but also grow more crops per year.

No growing media is needed with aeroponics. You can use baskets or closed cell foam plugs (compress around the plant's stem) to suspend the plants. These tools fit in the small holes on top of the growing chamber. In the growing chamber, the mist nozzles will spray the nutrient solution to the plant roots at short intervals. This regular spray has benefits of keeping the roots moist and provide the nutrients they need.

The growing chambers should be airtight and light proof (to prevent the root zone being penetrated by lights and make algae cannot thrive). It must allow air to get in for the growth of plant roots but you also don't want pests to get in or water to spill out. The chamber needs to be able to hold in the humidity as well. The ultimate factor which creates a successful aeroponic system is a balance of plenty of moisture, nutrients and fresh oxygen that you can provide to the roots.

Finally, a major factor which contributes to the success of this system is the water droplet size. A fine mist would create much faster-growing and bushier roots. These roots also have more surface area to absorb the oxygen and nutrients compared to those sprayed with small streams of water from small mist nozzles. This will also mean faster-growing plant canopy.

The Reservoir

This is where all your water and the nutrient solution will be stored. It's a closed-loop system, meaning whatever the plants don't absorb, gets dropped back into the reservoir to be re-sprayed until the plant roots absorb the water solution. The plants are never submerged in the water though. They're suspended in air using net cups as grow chambers.

Water/Nutrient Pump

Secured to the base of the reservoir is a water pump that's used to pump the water through the piping to the misting nozzles.

Repeat Cycle Timer

The repeat cycle timer is used to control the amount of water dispersed in the reservoir. If you research the recommended cycle times, you'll find growers having success with a misting cycle of one minute on and five minutes off, and others having similar successes on misting for 15-seconds and then off for up to five minutes.

There are no hard and fast rules as to what frequency you set your misting intervals. The important part is that you do set it, because otherwise, the roots will be drenched.

Your best bet is to test every new plant when you start out because the best cycle is the one that lets the plant roots nearly dry out before hitting them with another burst of atomized water.

Misting Nozzles

Different aeroponic systems will have a different number of misting nozzles used inside the chamber. These are an important part of the set up as the smaller the water droplet sprayed through the mister, the better the plant roots can absorb it.

A study by NASA research found that the best range is between 5 and 50 microns for the water droplets, which is the generally accepted standard for a high pressure aeroponics system. The finer the droplets the better the plants can absorb it.

Net Cups / Grow Chambers

Separating the plant roots from the plant tops is done using a lid with precisely cut holes to insert net cups that are used as grow chambers. These cups are inserted through the lid and sealed with (usually) a Styrofoam collar that provides both support for the stems and acts as a water barrier to keep the water contained in the reservoir.

All aeroponic systems have the same components and work the same way, but there are different types…

pH Level Consistency with Aeroponics Systems

The pH levels are super important in every hydroponic system. The reason being, the mist sprayed around the chamber cannot deliver everything a plant needs to grow. As the roots are suspended in air, there's plenty of oxygen going to be available.

In addition, the cycling of the water misters will create a constant humid environment, getting close to 100% humidity constantly, which is one of the main reasons aeroponics is so effective at growing robust plants.

However, in addition to the oxygen, there's essential minerals the plant is going to need that water alone cannot provide.

These include the essentials of:

Calcium

Nitrogen

Phosphorus

Potassium

Magnesium

Sulfur

The above are the main nutrients that need to be added to the water solution using a plant nutrient feed specifically designed to be used with aeroponic systems so that the roots can get all the nourishment they need for healthy growth.

Soil Test

In addition to added nutrition for the plants, there's the issue of pH, which is a measurement of acidity.

This needs to be just right for each plant. Deionized/distilled water has a neutral pH of 7, but the ideal pH for aeroponic systems leans more on the acidic side of the pH spectrum, requiring a pH of 6.

This doesn't need to be exact, so long as it stays above 5.0 and below 7.0, the roots will do okay.

A pH of 6 is ideal.

It's also worth noting that a lot of plant watering advice emphasizes rainwater as being preferential. That it is. But, you also need to know that not all rainwater has the same pH, or nutrient value because of environmental factors.

Someone living rurally will have cleaner rainwater than someone living in Massachusetts, which has the highest rainwater acidity (pH of 4.1) of 15 states East of the Mississippi. On average, rainwater is slightly acidic with a pH of 5.6, but that will vary by region.

There are a few ways to test your pH levels with the most accurate being a digital pH meter. The cheapest method is just to use paper strip tests, but you will need to consistently monitor the pH of your water, so in the long run, it's more cost effective to use a digital pH meter.

The other method is to use liquid pH tests. The digital meter is a one-off cost that you can buy once and use repeatedly.

As a LPA system is closed-loop, the water will recycle until the plant roots absorb it. Eventually, the reservoir will need topped up and when you do that, since regular water is more acidic than is preferred for aeroponics, you'll need to use pH adjusters to maintain the consistency.

You can find a pH up and down solution on Amazon.

Using these, you can get your water and the liquid plant feed to the optimal pH of 6.0 and maintain it throughout the grow cycle of each of your plants.

Monitoring EC levels in Your Reservoir

EC stands for Electrical Conductivity and it can tell you a lot about how your plant is growing. Not just what's in your reservoir, but how your plants are using what's available.

Plants are smart creatures. They only absorb what they need. In warmer months, they may take in more water than they do any other nutrients. When the temperatures are cooler, they can take in more of the nutrient solution than they do the water.

Because of this, if your water temperatures aren't maintained at a consistent level, you can find the pH levels alter, especially if your plants take in more water than the nutrients in the water.

When plants take in more nutrients than they do water, you could find leaf-burn becomes an issue. If on the other hand, more water is being absorbed than the nutrients, it's going to slow down the plant's growth rate.

Plants grow more healthily and faster when the EC is maintained at a consistent level. If during a cycle, you find the EC readings are lower than before, then the plant isn't taking in enough nutrients or the solution you're using isn't strong enough. When the EC readings go higher, the nutrient solution is too strong and would need diluting.

Now, the tricky part is keeping the pH and EC consistent because the readings will alter every time you refill the reservoir due to the water starting out acidic before nutrients are added.

EC readings should be taken daily to make sure it stays the same and when they aren't, nutrients should be added or the water diluted. Once a week or up to a fortnight, the reservoir should be cleaned and refilled with the right dilution of nutrient solution.

The reason being, if you don't, different minerals such as copper and zinc can accumulate in the tank causing deficiencies.

Regular cleaning of the tank is a preventative measure to keep your grow healthy. During the week if there are changes, that's when pH balancers (pH up and pH down solutions) can be used to tweak the nutrient solution being sprayed through the misters.

Just like the pH digital meters, you can use EC meters to measure the conductivity levels.

Now, because nutrients are delivering minerals into the water, it's going to create salt and this is where you really need to maintain your system because if you don't, the misters will get clogged causing the pump to work harder than it needs to.

Eventually, the entire system can be compromised because when there's too high a salt level, it can clog your pipes and sprinklers and stop delivering any nutrients to your plants.

If that does happen, because the roots are suspended in air relying on oxygen, humidity and a constant supply of nutrient-enriched water, a failure can see plants die fast.

These aren't like any other growing method where you can be lax with watering. Once the water stops being pumped effectively, the plants are compromised and often can be ruined. That's why they need a lot of monitoring.

Not so much care, but more about keeping an eye on your readings to spot potential problems before they become a problem.

Different plants have different nutritional needs. If you know the EC range for the type of plant you're growing, all you need to do is keep an eye on the readings to keep the conductivity within that range.

Aeroponics Troubleshooting

When you're growing with aeroponics, there's not much you can do manually to treat plant problems because everything is entirely reliant on the system working properly.

Any issues of plant growth, fungi appearing on plant foliage or roots, or even leaf burn, will be because of an issue with your system.

The most common problems with aeroponics are:

Pump malfunctions

Meet your worst nightmare. To put this in the simplest terms, don't skimp on your water pump. Cheap pumps really are nasty with an aeroponic system because the life of your crops relies on this working.

Inside the reservoir tank is close to 100% humidity level – when the pump is working. The water pump is the reason for high humidity. When that stops working, humidity drops fast.

Combine the fast humidity drop along with the fact the pump won't be able to spray any nutrients to the plant, the plant roots are then starved, which is why there's a likelihood of your plants dying if the pump packs in.

The life of your plants relies on the water pump working. The instant it stops, there's a serious problem.

Blocked nozzles

This is an easy one to miss and it's also an easy fix. You see, with all the nutrients in the water being sprayed through the nozzles, those minerals will accumulate salt. Eventually, the salt molecules can accumulate in the pipes, reaching the nozzles at which point they'll block it.

A partial blockage will slow down the misting, whereas a full nozzle blockage will stop any mist being sprayed. For that reason, it's best to regularly check your nozzles are working as they should be.

If they aren't, the only solution you need is isopropyl – aka, rubbing alcohol. Just rub it over the nozzles and it'll get to work breaking down the salt molecules and getting your nozzles unblocked fairly quickly.

Multiple Problems with bacteria and fungi – The One Solution Fix

If you've done any research into the pros and cons of aeroponics, you'll no doubt be aware of bacteria and fungi being of a higher probability than any other growing method.

Well, that's just not true. What is fact is that all the conditions bacteria and fungi need to grow and spread rapidly are present in the reservoir of an aeroponic system. Warm temperatures and a humid environment.

The truth is, there's no more bacteria or fungi concerns with aeroponics other than one and that's Pythium Root Rot. The only reason is because the Pythium disease has a spore that can swim, meaning once it's present in your reservoir, it's going to infect all the water, and be dispersed onto the plants with every spray of the jets.

There's only one thing you can do here and that's prevention because if you do get disease ridden water, your plants will have seen their day.

Hydrogen Peroxide is the solution to fixing all the concerns to do with bacteria and fungi and that's because on contact, it'll eradicate it.

It also brings a new problem to the table and that's the fact it's so strong it can kill your plants, so while you're trying to protect your crops, you could actually risk killing them yourself.

You need to get the dilution part just right, which is even trickier than you'd imagine because the majority of hydrogen peroxide suppliers already dilute what they sell to you.

Food grade is the best you can use since most of your plants will be of the editable type. That's 35% and there's very few manufacturers certified to supply this high a grade of hydrogen peroxide.

The recommended amount of peroxide to use in your reservoir is 3% per gallon to last up to four days. If you're working in liters, it's just 3ml per 1 liter of water. Remember to use the 3% peroxide solution.

At this concentration, your plants will be protected against a variety of bacteria, pests and viruses.

Maintaining Your Aeroponic System

The reservoir is where you need to pay the most attention to for maintenance but don't neglect your grow room.

Two words to remember to grow healthy crops with aeroponics are "sanitize and sterilize."

Cleaning

1 – Sanitize

Everything around your grow room needs to be kept clean, dust free and free of anything that's going to encourage any bacteria growth. For cleaning, treat your grow room as your kitchen. If anything is spilled, clean it up.

For your plant foliage, you'll want to keep those healthy by trimming off dead leaves, maintaining the temperatures and ensuring the right amount of light is reaching the plant foliage.

2 – Sterilize

The key area to keep sterile is your reservoir. You'll also have the irrigation system (piping delivering the water) to keep sterile, ensuring there's not too high a salt build-up that could block nozzles and decrease the system's efficiency.

For this, hydrogen peroxide is the best solution you can use to keep your reservoir sterile while it's operating. Between grows, that's a different matter that's addressed by a cleaning flush.

A cleaning flush will involve completely sterilizing the system using bleach or similar cleaning agents. A scrubbing brush is best used to make sure you're getting into every crevice within the reservoir.

Once you've thoroughly cleaned what you can, then run the system with a diluted bleach solution so that the piping, and the jet nozzles get sterilized too.

Once your flush is done, you need to get rid of any chemicals you used to clean it by running the system with just water. Let the water get rid of any lingering chemicals then let oxygen do its part to dry everything before you put it to use again with your next grow.

Whilst the reservoir is the key area to keep sterile, any equipment you're using such as pruners should also be sterilized before using on your plants.

Just one snip with a pair of dirty pruners could introduce plant pests or diseases, such as using the same pruner on outdoor plants then snipping one of your plants in your aeroponics system with those before sterilizing them.

Maintaining your aeroponic system is easy when you know why you're taking each step you take. You're keeping your grow room/area clean and tidy (sanitized) to prevent pests from being attracted to the area or airborne pathogens to be introduced that could affect your system and plants.

Sterilizing all the parts in the reservoir and the tools you use to tend to your plants is being proactive instead of reacting to plant diseases, common pests or any viruses.

The Pros and Cons of Aeroponics

After covering what aeroponics involves, including the various technical aspects of this method of growing, to wrap up, here's a bite-size list of the advantages and the disadvantages of aeroponics to help you decide if it's a good choice for you.

Pros

Extremely fast plant growth.

Only a small area is needed to get started if you use a vertical grow system.

Less nutrients are used because it's a closed-loop system. What your plants don't use, drops back into the reservoir to be cycled through the system. Nutrients and water are in constant supply and your plants will only use what they need, when they need it – day or night as it runs 24/7.

Ability to control the growing climate right down to knowing your plants are taking in the same amount of water as they are nutrients.

Less worry about plant pests.

Less water is needed and far less watering as the system will re-purpose water that isn't absorbed by the roots of your plants.

Cons

Totally reliant on the system.

Growers need to be competent with numbers and accurate with measurements of plant feeds and any chemicals you're using such as hydrogen peroxide.

Regular checks needed for pH and EC levels.

The constant moist environment of the chamber is inviting to bacterial pathogens and fungi, so while you'll have less care to provide, you will have more inspecting to do to make sure your pH and EC levels are consistent and the reservoir is fungi and bacteria free.

In Closing

There are less disadvantages than there are advantages, but the downside is that those disadvantages are really strong. It's a high level of commitment so don't be fooled by thinking there's nearly double the upsides than there are downsides.

Depending how committed you are to trying aeroponics, it could set you back a few hundred dollars for a quality aeroponic system. If that doesn't work out, you could have one expensive mistake on your hands.

That being said, it is a high-risk high-reward scenario because when the system is controlled to perfection, you will get a higher quality of crops at a faster production rate and much healthier plants than many other growing methods because of the 24/7 oxygen and nutrient supply to the plant roots providing full nourishment throughout t-he growing cycle.

The History of Aeroponics

Simply put, aeroponics is a method of growing plants in a soilless environment with very little water. Basically, it's growing without earth. Despite this leap in advancement, aeroponics actually had a fairly slow start. Techniques for growing plants without soil were first developed in the 1920s by botanists who used primitive aeroponi-cs to study plant root structure [source: Barak, et al]. This absence of soil made study much easier: In aeroponics, plants' roots dangle in midair, with only the plants' stems held in place. However, the leap in logic that led to growing plants in this way for recreation rather than academic study didn't occur until the 1970s. Hydroponics, a similar technology where plants' roots are grown in nutrient-rich water rather than soil, emerged and overtook aeroponic development.

Hydroponics (growing roots in a nutrient rich, water-based medium instead of soil) came into popular use in the West in the 1970s. Research and use of aeroponic systems continued behind the scenes, however, and the technique made its big public debut when "The Land" pavilion at Disney's Epcot Center opened in 1982.

It would take the interest of NASA to push aeroponics further into the limelight. In the 1990s, study and refinement of these techniques took off after NASA funded a project by a small aeroponics operation. NASA's involvement would give the growing aeroponics movement a decidedly futuristic image.

Aeroponic History - the beginning

Aeroponics International's patent for an Aeroponic method and apparatus, developed by

Richard Stoner, Founder and President, for greenhouse and nursery crop production. It utilizes an enclosed pulsed application of a hydro-atomized nutrient mist for rapid propagation of plants from cuttings. This Aeroponic technology was originally marketed in 1983 by Genisis Technology, of Boulder, CO. There are over 1,500 installations of the Genisis Aeroponic technology worldwide. Stoner left Genisis in 1986 and acquired the patent rights in 1988.

Aeroponic System Advancements

The original Genesis Aeroponic System has been significantly improved and redesigned for multi-crop production by Stoner since 1989. The improvements included virtually replace in-vitro and greenhouse mini tuber and crop production.

Micro propagation specialists and other plant scientists who have observed this "new generation" of Aeroponic rapid plant biotechnology, named RPB by Aeroponic International, concur that it represents a novel and totally new approach to crop production and research. For example, the implications for the potato industry utilizing RPB is expected to be 600% to 1400% more productive per sq. ft. compared to current tissue culture/greenhouse micro propagation.

Aeroponics International has also developed a modified version of RPB, offered as the Genesis Series III Aeroponic System.

Commercial aeroponics only took off during the 1980s, but has been growing ever since, because the need is clear – People are always looking for better and more convenient ways to grow plants with a minimum of fuss.

A guy named R. Stoner is generally credited with promoting commercial aeroponics worldwide by developing user friendly aeroponic systems, so much so that US space agency NASA has adopted many of his ideas, and are now one of the strongest proponents of aeroponics. Today, aeroponic systems are more "plug-and-play" than ever before, for the average Joe gardener, although still by no means brain dead easy to setup and maintain.

Some of the key benefits of aeroponics:

An aeroponic system by AeroGrowFast plant growth – The chief feature of aeroponics. Plants grow fast because their roots have access to a lot of oxygen 24/7.

Easy system maintenance – In aeroponics, all you need to maintain is the root chamber (the container housing the roots) which needs regular disinfecting, and periodically, the reservoir and irrigation channels. The constant semi-moist environment of the root chamber which invites bacterial growth is the only main drawback of all aeroponic system maintenance.

Less need for nutrients and water – Aeroponic plants need less nutrients and water on average, because the nutrient absorption rate is higher, and plants usually respond to aeroponic systems by growing even more roots.

Mobility – Plants, even whole nurseries, can be moved around without too much effort, as all that is required is moving the plants from one collar to another.

Requires little space – You don't need much space to start an aeroponics garden. Depending on the system, plants can be stacked up one on top of each other. Aeroponics is basically a modular system, which is perfect for maxing out limited space.

Great educational value – You can learn a great deal about plants from aeroponics. Kids especially will love having a small aeroponic system to grow a pet plant, without having to get their hands dirty.

Key disadvantages of aeroponics

Dependence on the system – A typical aeroponics system is made up of high pressure pumps, sprinklers and timers. If any of these break down, your plants can be damaged or killed easily.

Technical knowledge required – You need a certain level of competency in running an aeroponic system. Knowledge of nutrients amounts required by your plant is essential, because you don't have any soil to absorb excess/wrong nutrients supplied.

Regular cleaning of the root chamber – The root chamber must not be contaminated, or else diseases may strike the roots. So you need to disinfect the root chamber every so often. Hydrogen peroxide is often used as disinfectant.

High cost – Most aeroponic systems are not exactly cheap. Aeroponic systems may cost many hundreds of dollars each. The most affordable one I noticed, is still the one by (affiliatelink) AeroGrow, a unique form of commercial "aeroponics." Edit – Some folks point out that AeroGrow is not aeroponics – I think it is still a great system for small premises.

Plants are often grown aeroponically via a tower system.

In conclusion, aeroponics is still a good way to learn how to master plant growth and learn about their needs, within a controlled environment. For urban dwellers who live in apartments, sometimes aeroponics is the only practical way to garden. For budding farm ventures in high value crops, the cost of setting up an aeroponic nursery may turn out to be cheaper than acquiring a large plot of land to farm on. And on arid lands, aeroponics circumvents this problem, and provides the best means of growing plants effectively.

CHAPTER TWO
Vertical Farming

Our ancestors first learned to farm nearly 12,000 years ago. By cultivating and domesticating seeds, these once hunter-gatherers broke away from their nomadic lifestyles, settled down to produce controlled and reliable food sources (weather permitting, of course) and, little did they know, change the course of the planet's future.

Fast forward to the 20th century when a group of architects started planning to alter food production in their own way. They aimed to decreased dependency on traditional land-based farms and harness spatial efficiency in our dense built environment; think less wide-open spaces with tractors and more structures growing stacked layers of crops. This practice—widely referred to as "indoor" or "vertical farming" (taken from Gilbert Ellis Bailey's 1915 book of the same name)—is alive and booming today, and especially in the New York metro area.

Columbia University professor emeritus and ecologist Dickson Despommier helped to envision the modern vertical farm and indoor agriculture while teaching a graduate-level course in 1999. His students realized that simply using rooftop gardens would been grossly insufficient to feeding the population of Manhattan so in line with urban agriculture predecessors, he began researching different techniques and structures. Despommier is among several academics and vertical farming thought leaders who see vertical farming today as part of the answer to a range of global problems (many partly caused by agriculture) including climate change and water scarcity.

There are a lot of ways to farm indoors and below are three different soilless processes recommended by Despommier. Done properly at various scales, they're as effective as at growing crops in skyscrapers as they are in 500 square foot studio apartments:

Hydroponics

One of the oldest and most common methods of vertical farming, hydroponics includes growing plants without soil and in a water solvent containing mineral nutrients. The simplest hydroponic method (called the floating raft system) suspends the plants in soilless raft like a polystyrene sheet and lets the roots hang to absorb the oxygen-aerated solution. Another common method is the nutrient film technique, which is popular for growing lettuce. Here, a stream of the nutrient-dissolved solution is pumped into an angled channel, typically a plastic pipe, containing the plants. This runs past the plants' root mat and can then be recirculated for continuous use. New York's Gotham Greens and Square Roots use hydroponics.

Aeroponics

It's no surprise that NASA has been backing research on aeroponic growth for the past two decades as it's free-floating-roots aesthetic is typically used in futuristic sci-fi movies. With aeroponics, the dangling roots absorb a fine mist comprised of an atomized version of the nutrient solution sprayed directly onto the roots by a pump. Although aeroponics enables plants to grow much more quickly than hydroponics, it requires more solution and therefore is more costly. Newark's Aerofarms uses aeroponics.

Aquaponics

Like hydroponic systems, an aquaponic system contains a soil-free plant bed suspended over a body of water containing nutrients necessary for plant growth. But within the body of water is a population of fish (typically herbivores) that produce waste that function as fertilizer for the plants. In turn, the plants help purify the water to make the water suitable for the fish.

Given that a balance must be achieved to ensure the system of both life forms, aquaponics requires greater attention than hydroponics or aeroponics although filtration and aeration systems can help manage these complications. Furthermore, the types of plants one can grow are much more limited as the necessary plant nutrients must be compatible with those necessary for the fish.

Rationale for Vertical Farms

The advent of agriculture has ushered in an unprecedented increase in the human population and their domesticated animals. Farming catalyzed our transformation from primitive hunter-gatherers to sophisticated urban dwellers in just 10,000 years. Today, over 800 million hectares is committed to soil-based agriculture, or about 38% of the total landmass of the earth. It has re-arranged the landscape in favor of cultivated fields at the expense of natural ecosystems, reducing most natural areas to fragmented, semi-functional units, while completely eliminating many others. A reliable food supply was the result. This singular invention has facilitated our growth as a species to the point now of world domination over the natural world from which we evolved. Despite the obvious advantage of not having to hunt or scavenge for our next meal, farming has led to new health hazards by creating ecotones between the natural world and our cultivated fields. As the result, transmission rates of numerous infectious disease agents have dramatically increased- influenza, rabies, yellow fever, dengue fever, malaria, trypanosomiasis, hookworm, schistosomiasis – and today these agents emerge and re-emerge with devastating regularity at the tropical and sub-tropical agricultural interface. Modern agriculture employs a multitude of chemical products, and exposure to toxic levels of some classes of agrochemicals (pesticides, fungicides) have created other significant health risks that are only now being sorted out by epidemiologists and toxicologists. As if that were no enough to be concerned about, it is predicted that over the next 50 years, the human population is expected to rise to at least 8.6 billion, requiring an additional 109 hectares to feed them using current technologies, or roughly the size of Brazil. That quantity of additional arable land is simply not available. Without an alternative strategy for dealing with just this one problem, social chaos will surely replace orderly behavior in most over-crowded countries. Novel ways for obtaining an abundant and varied food supply without encroachment into the few remaining functional ecosystems must be seriously entertained. One solution involves the construction of urban food production centers – vertical farms – in which our food would be continuously grown inside of tall buildings within the built environment. If we could engineer this approach to food production, then no crops would ever fail due to severe weather events (floods, droughts, hurricanes, etc.). Produce would be available to city dwellers without the need to transport it thousands of miles from rural farms to city markets. Spoilage would be greatly reduced, since crops would be sold and consumed within moments after harvesting. If vertical farming in urban centers becomes the norm, then one anticipated long-term benefit would be the gradual repair of many of the world's damaged ecosystems through the systematic abandonment of farmland. In temperate and tropical zones, the re-growth of hardwood forests could play a significant role in carbon sequestration and may help reverse current trends in global climate change. Other benefits of vertical farming include the creation of a sustainable urban environment that encourages good health for all who choose to live there; new employment opportunities, fewer abandoned lots and buildings, cleaner air, safe use of municipal liquid waste, and an abundant supply of safe drinking water.

As of 2004, approximately 800 million hectares of land were in use for food production – approximating an area equivalent to Brazil, and allowing for the harvesting of an ample food supply for the majority of a human population approaching 6.3 billion. These land-use estimates include grazing lands (formerly grasslands) for cattle, and represents nearly 85% of all land that can support at least a minimum level of agricultural activity. In addition, farming produces a wide variety of feed grains for many millions of head of cattle and other species of domesticated farm animal. In 2003, nearly 33 million head of cattle were produced in the United States, alone In order to support this large a scale of agricultural activity, millions of hectares of hardwood forest (temperate and tropical), grasslands, wetlands, estuaries, and to a lesser extent coral reefs have been either eliminated or severely damaged with significant loss of biodiversity and wide-spread disruption of ecosystem functions.

The advantages of farming are obvious enough from a human perspective, but even our earliest efforts caused irreversible damage to the land. For example, some

8,000 to 10,000 years ago, the fertile, silt-laden soils of the floodplains of the Tigris and Euphrates River valleys were rapidly degraded below minimum food production limits due to erosion caused by intensive farming and mis-managed irrigation projects that were often interrupted by wars and out-of-season flooding events. Today, primitive farming practices continue to produce massive loss of topsoil, while excluding the possibility for long-term carbon sequestration in the form of trees and other permanent woods plants. Agrochemicals, particularly fertilizers, are used in almost every major farming system regardless of location, largely due to the demand, year in and year out, for cash crops that extract more nutrients from the substrate that it can provide. Mono-crops are extraordinarily vulnerable to a wide range of insect pests and microbial disease agents due to the very nature of farming (i.e., growing large numbers of a given plant species in a confined area). To mount a counter-offensive, we have invented pesticides and herbicides. Their use has become routine in many situations, particularly in factory farms. Agricultural runoff, which typically contains all of the above-mentioned classes of chemicals, and is also often laden with unhealthy levels of heavy metals, as well, is generally acknowledged as the most pervasive and destructive form of water pollution, degrading virtually every freshwater aquatic environment that borders on human habitation.

Many of the earth's most impacted regions (i.e., those with the highest population densities) are generally conceded to be unhealthy places to live (western Europe and North America excepted), with infant morbidity/mortality rates many times greater than those found in Europe and North America. These are the same places from which new kinds of emerging and known varieties of re-emerging infections are found. Many of them are zoonotic and their life cycles would not normally include humans were it not for encroachment, an activity driven by the need to expand farming into the natural landscape. Nonetheless, there is at present a wide variety of produce available, and in quantity, for those that can afford it. Ironically, many millions of people living predominantly throughout the tropics and sub-tropics are severely malnourished, while living within countries many of which export large amounts of agricultural products destined for the markets of the developed world.

Farming is an occupation fraught with a wide variety of health risks. Numerous infectious disease agents (e.g., schistosomes, malaria, geohelminths) take advantage of a wide variety of traditional agricultural practices (irrigation, plowing, sowing, harvesting), facilitating their transmission. These diseases take a huge toll on human health, disabling large populations, thus removing them from the flow of commerce, even in the poorest of countries. Other health risks to farmers include acute exposure to toxic agrochemicals (e.g., pesticides and fungicides), bites from noxious wildlife, and trauma injuries. The latter two risk categories are particularly common among "slash and burn" subsistence farmers. It is reasonable to expect that as the human population continues to grow, so do these problems.

Consensus among demographers regarding estimates of the rate at which the global human population will increase is difficult to achieve, but most agree that over the next 50 years, the number will increase to at least

9.2 billion. It is also conceded by some of the worlds' leading agronomists that they will require an additional10 9 hectares of land (roughly the size of Brazil) if they are to produce enough food by conventional methods to meet their needs. Since there is essentially no high quality land remaining for this purpose, it seems obvious that a major crisis of global proportion may well be looming on the very near horizon. Limited resources (food, water, and shelter) are some of the major causes for civil unrest and war throughout the world.

Vertical farming practiced on a large scale in urban centers has great potential to: 1. supply enough food in a sustainable fashion to comfortably feed all of humankind for the foreseeable future; 2. allow large tracts of land to revert to the natural landscape restoring ecosystem functions and services; 3. safely and efficiently use the organic portion of human and agricultural waste to produce energy through methane generation, and at the same time significantly reduce populations of vermin (e.g., rats, cockroaches); 4. remediate black water creating a much needed new strategy for the conservation of drinking water; 5. take advantage of abandoned and unused urban spaces; 6. break the transmission cycle of agents of disease associated with a fecally-contaminated environment; 7. allow year-round food production without loss of yields due to climate change or weather-related events; 8. eliminate the need for large-scale use of pesticides and herbicides; 9. provide a major new role for agrochemical industries (i.e., designing and producing safe, chemically-defined diets for a wide variety of commercially viable plant species; 10. create an environment that encourages sustainable urban life, promoting a state of good health for all those who choose to live in cities. All of this may sound too good to be true, but careful analysis will show that these are all realistic and achievable goals, given the full development of a few new technologies.

High-rise food-producing building will succeed only if they function by mimicking ecological process, namely by safely and efficiently re-cycling everything organic, and re-cycling water from human waste disposal plants, turning it back into drinking water. Most important, there must be strong, government-supported economic incentives to the private sector, as well as to universities and local government to develop the concept. Ideally, vertical farms must be: a. cheap to build; b. durable and safe to operate; and c. independent of economic subsides and outside support (i.e., show a profit at the end of the day). If these conditions can be realized through an on-going, comprehensive research program, urban agriculture could provide an abundant and varied food supply for the 60% of the people that will be living within cities by the year 2030. This migration is largely caused by the plight of the farmer. " People move to the city for various reasons, but the most significant reason is economic—when a city's economy is prospering it attracts people. The promise of jobs and comfort, glamour and glitter, "pulls" people to cities. There are also "push" factors: droughts or exploitation of farmers can cause extreme rural poverty and that "pushes" people out of the country-side".

What is meant by vertical farming?

Farming indoors is not a new concept, per se, as greenhouse-based agriculture has been in existence for some time. Numerous commercially viable crops (e.g., strawberries, tomatoes, peppers, cucumbers, herbs, and spices) have seen their way to the world's supermarkets in ever increasing amounts over the last 15 years. Most of these operations are small when compared to factory farms, but unlike their outdoor counterparts, these facilities can produce crops year-round. Japan, Scandinavia, New Zealand, the United States, and Canada have thriving greenhouse industries. As far as is known, none have been constructed as multi-story buildings. Other food items that have been commercialized by indoor farming include freshwater fishes (e.g., tilapia, trout, stripped bass), and a wide variety of crustaceans and mollusks (e.g., shrimp, crayfish, mussels).

What is proposed here that differs radically from what now exists is to scale up the concept of indoor farming, in which a wide variety of produce is harvested in quantity enough to sustain even the largest of cities without significantly relying on resources beyond the city limits. Cattle, horses, sheep, goats, and other large farm animals seem to fall well outside the paradigm of urban farming. However, raising a wide variety of fowl and pigs are well within the capabilities of indoor farming. It has been estimated that it will require approximately 300 square feet of intensively farmed indoor space to produce enough food to support a single individual living in an extraterrestrial environment (e.g., on a space station or a colony on the moon or Mars)(35). Working within the framework of these calculations, one vertical farm with an architectural footprint of one square city block and rising up to 30 stories (approximately 3 million square feet) could provide enough nutrition (2,000 calories/day/person) to comfortably accommodate the needs of 10,000 people employing technologies currently available. Constructing the ideal vertical farm with a far greater yield per square foot will require additional research in many areas – hydrobiology, engineering, industrial microbiology, plant and animal genetics, architecture and design, public health, waste management, physics, and urban planning, to name but a few. The vertical farm is a theoretical construct whose time has arrived, for to fail to produce them in quantity for the world at-large in the near future will surely exacerbate the race for the limited amount of remaining natural resources of an already stressed out planet, creating an intolerable social climate.

Expected benefits of vertical farming

Year-round crop production in a protected, managed environment:

Currently, maximizing crop production takes place over an annual growth cycle that is wholly dependent upon what happens outside – climate and local weather conditions. Despite recent advances in predicting the occurrence of these natural processes by an extensive network of ground-based weather stations and remote sensing satellites, 2-dimensional farming remains a precarious way to make a living. Significant deviation (e.g., drought or flood) for more than several weeks from conditions necessary for insuring a good yield has predictable, negative effects on the lives of millions of people dependent upon those items for their yearly food supply. Climate change regimens will surely complicate an already complex picture with respect to predicting crop yields.

In addition, other elements conspire to take away from the harvest for which we worked so hard to produce. Despite the best application of modern agricultural practices, an unavoidable portion of what is grown rots in the fields prior to harvest time, or in the world's storage bins afterwards. Every year, depending upon geographic location and intensity of El Niño events, crops suffer from too little water and wither on the spot, or are lost to severe flooding, hailstorms, tornados, earthquakes, hurricanes, cyclones, fires, and other destructive events of nature. Many of these phenomena are at best difficult to predict, and at worst are impossible to react to in time to prevent the losses associated with them. In sub-Saharan Africa, locusts remain an ever-present threat, and can devastate vast areas of farmland in a matter of days. Even after a bumper crop is realized, problems associated with processing and storage lessen the actual tonnage that is available to the consumer. A large portion of the harvest, regardless of the kind of plant or grain, is despoiled or a portion consumed by a variety of opportunistic life forms (i.e., fungi, bacteria, insects, rodents) after being stored. While it is conceded that at present the abundance of cash crops is more than sufficient to meet the nutritional needs of the world's human population, delivering them to world markets is driven largely by economics, not biological need. Thus, the poorest people – some 1.1 billion – are forced to live in a constant state of starvation, with many thousands of deaths per year attributable to this wholly preventable predicament. Locating vertical farms near these human "hot spots" would greatly alleviate this problem.

Vertical farming (i.e., faming in three dimensions) promises to eliminate external natural processes as confounding elements in the production of food, since crops will be grown indoors under carefully selected and well-monitored conditions, insuring an optimal growth rate for each species of plant and animal year round. It is estimated that one acre of vertical farm could be equivalent to as many as ten to twenty traditional soil-based acres, depending upon which crop species is considered. Growing food close to home will lower significantly the amount of fossil fuels needed to deliver them to the consumer, and will eliminate forever the need for fossil fuels during the act of farming (i.e., plowing, applying fertilizer, seeding, weeding, harvesting).

Advantages of Vertical Farming

Year-round crop production

Eliminates agricultural runoff

Significantly reduces use of fossil fuels (farm machines and transport of crops)

Makes use of abandoned or unused properties

No weather related crop failures

Offers the possibility of sustainability for urban centers

Converts black and gray water to drinking water

Adds energy back to the grid via methane generation

Creates new urban employment opportunities

Reduces the risk of infection from agents transmitted at the agricultural interface

Returns farmland to nature, helping to restore ecosystem functions and services

Controls vermin by using restaurant waste for methane generation

No-cost restoration of ecosystems: the principle of "benign neglect"

Proof of concept:

The best reason to consider converting most food production to vertical farming is the promise of restoring ecosystem services and functions. There is good reason to believe that an almost full recovery of many of the world's endangered terrestrial ecosystems will occur simply by abandoning a given area of encroachment and allowing the land to "cure" itself. This belief stems, in part, from numerous anecdotal observations as to the current biological state of some territories that were once severely damaged either by now-extinct civilizations or over-farming, and, in part, from data derived from National Science Foundation-sponsored long-term ecological research program (LTER), begun in 1980, on a wide variety of fragmented ecosystems purposely set aside subsequent to an extended period of encroachment. The following case studies will serve to illustrate these points.

Deforestation of vast tracts of tropical rainforest throughout Mesoamerica took place over several thousand years. It is estimated that there were as many as 50 million people living in this region, with some 17 million in Mexico, alone, when the conquistadores arrived in the 1500s. Re-forestation of deserted regions previously inhabited by pre-Colombian civilizations (e.g., Mayans) began during the Spanish imperial venture and continued on after it failed. Regions that remained populated continued to suffer the ecological consequences of deforestation (ibid), but in the abandoned areas the re-growth of the rainforests in some parts of Central America was so complete that by 1950 nearly all of the major ancient cities and monuments lying between Panama and southern Mexico had been canopied under them. Today, archaeological expeditions routinely discover previously unknown settlements and the life and times of the peoples that lived there, but they are hard-won victories, accompanied by much difficulty in navigating the dense growth that protect these treasures of the past from open view. New finds are now often aided by sophisticated remote sensing technologies.

Along the northern border of the Brazilian jungle live the Yanomami. These people have never been conquered by European colonialists. Left to evolve on their own without interference from the outside, they have formed a series of loosely knit tribes that have developed shifting agricultural methods to live off the land, mostly by hunting bush meat and subsistence farming, without causing permanent damage to the environment in which they must live. Their farming methods do not include fire as a forest clearing mechanism. Instead, they cut down the trees, creating large open circles. Then they burn the trees to get enough minerals to fertilize the cleared zone. They farm the nutrient-poor soils for several years, raising sweet potatoes, plantains, sugar cane, and tobacco, and then they move on. By the time the Yanomami return to the same farming locale, some years later, the area has re-grown to its former state. Without fire as a confounding factor, the Yanomami have achieved a rare a balance with the land in which crops are produced and forestland is repaired by a natural cycle that favors the survival of both sets of life forms. Many other cultures living close to the land were not as fortunate as the Yanomami to have conceived and implemented sustainable relationships with their surroundings and have paid the ultimate price, that of extinction.

The "dust bowl" was created by farming in what was formerly short and tall grasslands prairie in the central Great Plains of the United States (portions of Kansas, Colorado, Oklahoma, and Texas). This represents one of

the best-documented examples of how misuse of land
not at all suited for traditional farming, coupled with a
100-year drought that affected nearly 2/3rds of the
country, resulted in the seemingly irreversible collapse
of a diverse assemblage of plants and animals adapted
to that semi arid environment. Between 1889-1895, a
total of 6 land rushes were sponsored by the
government, at the insistence of the "Boomers", to
jump start settlement of the Oklahoma territories. They
attracted thousands of hopeful immigrants from the
eastern United States and Europe to that area of the
west. Over the next 20 years, rainfall was above average
and farming flourished. However, the next 20-30 years
saw some of the worst droughts in recorded history for
that region. The result was a systematic erosion of
millions of tons of topsoil. The situation intensified from
1932-1938 with increasingly devastating results. During
that short time, all farming ceased and thousands of
families abandoned the land and headed further west,
mostly to California, in search of a better life (re-John
Steinbeck's Grapes of Wrath). The weather patterns had
conspired to defeat these early settlers in their quest to
re-shape the landscape into productive farmland.

Lesions learned, no one returned to the dust bowl region for some 15 years. During the intervening period, nurturing precipitation regimens returned, and the assemblages of wildlife long absent re-populated the region. Tall and short grasses re-built the soil enough to attract back the kit fox, antelope, prairie dog, and a wide variety of endemic birds and other support plants, reclaiming their niches and restoring the region to a mixed grasslands prairie. Seeds of native plants that had lain dormant germinated and thrived when competition with cash crop species for limited resources ceased. Following WWII, the area once again suffered ecological loss from the impacts of farming. This time that activity was supported by groundwater pumped from the Ogallala aquifer for irrigation of wheat, which requires additional water to achieve maximum yield. However, this initiative, too, will apparently fail soon for the same reason that the first wave of farming on the Great Plains did, namely the lack of a reliable source of freshwater. In this case, too much groundwater has already been drawn off, lowering the water table and resulting in an economic conundrum, where the price of oil, a necessary ingredient to fuel the heavy-duty pumps needed to raise water from a greater depth than at present (currently fueled by cheaper natural gas-driven pumps), will not prove to be cost-effective with respect to the price of wheat. It is anticipated that when this generation of farmers abandons the land, the prairie will once again dominate the landscape.

The de-militarized zone between North and South Korea represents a small strip of land some 1,528 km2 in area and off limits to people since the end of the Korean War in 1953. Farming communities once abundant there no longer till the soil. The result of abandonment has been striking, and in favor of ecological recovery. During the intervening years, remnant populations of wildlife have re-bounded into robust populations within that narrow region, including the Asiatic black bear, musk deer, and the red-crowned crane. An unexpected (and unwanted) example of "proof of concept", vivax malaria has also retuned to the area next to the DMZ in South Korea, as the result of that country's inability to carry out effective mosquito-control programs that would ordinarily include portions of the DMZ.

Today, we face the challenge of trying to understand enough about the process of ecological balance to incorporate it into our daily lives (i.e., do no harm). Our willingness to try to solve problems that we ourselves have created is a measure of our selflessness and altruistic behavior as a species. Thus, the second most important reason to consider converting to vertical farming relates to how we handle waste, and particularly that which comes from living in urban centers. Waste management throughout the world, regardless of location, is in most cases unacceptable, both from a public health and social perspective, and exposure to untreated effluent often carries with it serious health risks. However, even in the best of situations, most solid waste collections are simply compacted and relegated to landfills, or in a few instances, incinerated to generate energy. Liquid wastes are processed (digested, then de-sludged), then treated with a bactericidal agent (e.g., chlorine) and released into the nearest convenient body of water. More often in less developed countries, it is discarded without treatment, greatly increasing the health risks associated with infectious disease transmission due to fecal contamination.

All solid waste can be re-cycled (returnable cans, bottles, cardboard packages, etc.) and/or used in energy generating schemes with technologies that are currently in use. A major source of organic waste comes from the restaurant industry. Methane generation from this single resource could contribute significantly to energy generation, and may be able to supply enough to run vertical farms without the use of electricity from the grid. For example, in New York City there are more than 21,000 food service establishments, all of which produce significant quantities of organic waste, and they have to pay to have the city cart it off. Often the garbage sits out on the curb, sometimes for hours to days, prior to collection. This allows time for vermin (cockroaches, rats, mice) the privilege of dining out at some of the finest restaurants in the western hemisphere; albeit second-hand. Vertical farming may well result in a situation in which restaurants would be paid (according to the caloric content?) for this valuable commodity, allowing for a greater measure of income for an industry with a notoriously small (2-5%) profit margin. In New York City, on average 80-90 restaurants close down each year, the vast majority of which are precipitated by inspections conducted by the New York City Department of Health. A common finding by inspectors in these situations is vermin (mouse and rat droppings, cockroaches) and unsanitary conditions that encourage their life styles.

Agricultural runoff despoils vast amounts of surface and groundwater. Vertical farming offers the possibility of greatly reducing the quantity of this non-point source of water pollution. In addition, it will generate methane from municipal waste currently being funneled into water pollution control facilities. The concept of sustainability will be realized through the valuing of waste as a commodity so indispensable to the operation of the farm that to discard something —any thing — would be analogous to siphoning off a gallons' worth of gasoline from the family car and setting it on fire. Natural systems function in a sustainable fashion by recycling all essential elements needed to produce the next generation of life. This way of doing business is being incorporated by NASA engineers into all future programs that focus on colonizing outer space. If we are to live in closed systems off the surface of the earth, then the concept of waste becomes an outdated paradigm. Unfortunately, this goal has yet to be fully realized by NASA or by the ill-fated Biosphere 2 Project. If we are to live in a balanced extraterrestrial environment, we must somehow learn how to do it here first.

Sludge, derived from waste water treatment plants of many, but not all cities throughout the US, and treated with a patented process referred to as advanced alkaline stabilization with subsequent accelerated drying, is being turned into high grade topsoil and sold as such to the farming community at-large by N-Viro Corporation, Toledo, Ohio. The limiting factor in using municipal sludge for farming appears to be heavy metal contamination, mostly from copper, mercury, zinc, arsenic, and chromium. Vertical farms will be engineered to take in black or gray water, depending upon availability, and restore it to near drinking water quality using bioremediation and other technologies yet to be perfected. Fast growing inedible plant species (e.g., cattail, duckweed, sawgrass, Spartina spp.), often referred to collectively as a living machine will be used to help remediate contaminated water. They will be periodically harvested for methane generation employing state-of-the-art composting methods, yielding energy to help run the facility. By-products of burning methane – CO 2, heat, and water – can be added back into the atmosphere of the vertical farm to aid in fostering optimal plant growth. The resulting purified water will be used to grow edible plant species. Ultimately, any water source that emerges from the vertical farm should be drinkable, thus completely re-cycling it back into the community that brought it to the farm to begin with. Harvesting water generated from evapo-transpiration appears to have some virtue in this regard, since the entire farm will be enclosed. A cold brine pipe system could be engineered to aid in the condensation and harvesting of moisture released by plants. Nonetheless, several varieties of new technology will be needed before sewage can be handled in a routine, safe manner within the confines of the farm.

Lesions learned from the nuclear power plant industry should be helpful in this regard.

Social benefits of vertical farming

Eliminating a significant percentage of land dedicated to traditional farming has obvious health advantages regarding the restoration of ecosystem services, and for the immediate improvement of biodiversity by simultaneously restoring ecosystem functions, as well. The social benefits of urban agriculture promise an equally rewarding set of achievable goals. However, since the vertical farm is still a theoretical construct, it is difficult to predict all of the potential benefits that may arise from producing food in this manner. The first is the establishment of sustainability as an ethic for human behavior. At present, there are no examples of a totally sustained urban community anywhere in the world. The development of this keystone ecological concept has remained identified solely with the natural world, and specifically with reference to the functioning of ecosystems. Ecological observations and studies, beginning with those of Teal, show how life behaves with regards to the sharing of limited energy resources. Tight knit assemblages of plants and animals evolve into trophic relationships that allow for the seamless flow of energy transfer from one level to the next, regardless of the type of ecosystem in question (95). In fact, this is the defining characteristic of all ecosystems. In contrast, humans, although participants in all terrestrial ecosystems, have failed to incorporate this same behavior into their own lives. If vertical farming succeeds, it will establish the validity of sustainability, irrespective of location (urban vrs rural). Vertical farms could become important learning centers for generations of city-dwellers, demonstrating our intimate connectedness to the rest of the world by mimicking the nutrient cycles that once again take place in the world that has re-emerged around them. Furthermore, the elimination of large, currently unmanageable amounts of waste will improve the attractiveness of the local environment and help to correct the imbalance in energy utilization by recycling organic waste through methane digestion systems. Rene Dubos wrote in So Human an Animal that people tend to support the institutions that they grow up with, regardless of whether or not they foster a nurturing environment in which to live. Dubos advocated that all humans deserve to live in places that encourage healthy, useful lives, but that to do so will require massive reconstruction of the urban landscape. By transforming cities into entities that nurture the best aspects of the human experience is the goal of every city planner, and with vertical farming serving as a center-piece, this may eventually become a reality.

Providing all urban populations with a varied and plentiful harvest, tailored to the local cuisine eliminates food and water as resources that need to be won by conflict between competing populations. Starvation becomes a thing of the past, and the health of millions improves dramatically, largely due to proper nutrition and the lack of parasitic infections formerly acquired at the agricultural interface. Given the strength of resolve and insight at the political and social level, this concept has the potential to accomplish what has been viewed in the past as nearly impossible and highly impractical.

It is further anticipated that large-scale urban agriculture will be more labor-intensive than is currently practiced on the traditional farm scene, since the deployment of large farm machinery will not be an option. Hence, employment opportunities abound at many levels. Finally, the vertical farm should be a thing of architectural beauty as well as be highly functional, bringing a sense of pride to the neighborhoods in which they are built. In fact, the goal of vertical farm construction is to make them so desirable in all aspects that every neighborhood will want one for their very own.

CHAPTER THREE

Aeroponic towers:

Aeroponic towers are popular amongst start up growers and small scale commercial farmers. We spoke with a developer of the system to learn more about them. AGI Farms is a Florida-based company devoted to the sale of aeroponic towers; a system which, according to designer Richard Gittings, is oriented towards both residential and commercial customers. "On the residential side, we have the 'living pantry', which can be of any size, from just 32x32 inches to larger pantries with lights to grow indoors; commercial units are sold with previous knowledge about what the customer intends to grow."

To give an example, a grower interested in growing lettuce must take into account that the towers can accommodate 30 plant sites per ring, which "go three rings high, meaning 90 plant sites per tower. If he/she wants 1,000 heads of lettuce per week, we'll have ten towers per section. Lettuce will take 6 weeks from germination to the finished product, thus with 6 sections the grower will obtain those 1,000 heads," explains Richard.

There are many good reasons to grow a garden, any garden. However, there are special reasons for growing an aeroponic garden. We happen to have the Tower Garden by Juice Plus. But there are other great aeroponic systems available. However, we will refer to the Tower Garden. Some of these reasons will surprise you:

1. THE TOWER GARDEN IS AN INSTANT GARDEN

Gardeners are usually not after instant things. We love slow food, homegrown and homemade. But, if you really want to start gardening and the garden is not ready, or worse, the gardening season is 3 months away, the idea of an instant garden is very appealing.

The Tower Garden is just that: a garden that you can start growing instantly no matter what time of the year it is. The Tower Garden comes with everything you need to start growing right away. All you will need to add is water. Tap water and also rain water work great.

Before you even assemble the Tower Garden, start the seeds and start growing. Since hydroponics / aeroponics do not use any soil, we do not plant seeds in soil.

The Tower Garden comes with Rockwool starter cubes and Vermiculite to cover the seeds to keep them moist, as well as seeds and a seedling starting tray. Learn more following the link: Planting a Hydroponic Garden.

2. THE TOWER GARDEN IS A HIGH QUALITY PRODUCT

The Tower Garden is made from high-quality, USDA-approved, UV-stabilized, food-grade plastic. The quality is simply amazing. The garden is easy to assemble, to clean, and it simply works.

The Tower Garden is not just a garden, it is a growing system with many helpful accessories like a plant cage and grow lights that fit onto the cage. All of this makes successful growing easy.

Tower Tonic has rich, abundant, ionic earth minerals like nitrogen, phosphorus, potassium, calcium, magnesium, sulfur, and trace minerals, like boron, chlorine, manganese, and zinc that are important for plant growth. Rich in calcium, and rich in trace minerals that are important to people.

The Tower Tonic A and B is all you will need to grow leafy greens, as well as fruit bearing plants. There is no adjustment or twisting needed. It really does work, which leads us to #3.

3. TOWER GARDENING IS EASY

The Tower Garden vertical aeroponics growing system is a healthier, easier, smarter way to grow your own fresh and nutritious fruits, vegetables, and herbs.

Since there is no soil involved, there is also no weeding, no digging, and no bending over your garden. The well written out instruction manual will tell you all you need to know. However, like with any garden, I find learning by doing is best. Experience is what will make you into a great Tower Garden gardener. If you have never grown anything hydroponically, don't worry, with the Tower Garden and Tower Tonic it really is easy. But I would not call it a no work garden. You still need to care for the plants, and some of the work will remind you more of doing dishes than gardening.

4. THE TOWER GARDEN USES LITTLE SPACE FOR HIGH YIELD

The Tower Garden is a vertical aeroponics growing system. Growing vertically, the Tower Garden allows you to grow up to 28 plants. That's container gardening plus! 28 containers in less than six square feet of land. Using aeroponics and the specially formulated plant food, you can grow up to 30% more produce compared to traditional soil gardening during the same time period. This is is huge for short growing season gardeners.

5. THE TOWER GARDEN IS MOVABLE

Not just the Tower Garden dolly makes moving the garden easy, but you can actually carry the whole garden at any stage into a different location. Again, for short season growers it really adds up growing time. We can plant summer crops indoors without having to transplant them outdoors. We just carry out the whole garden when the weather conditions are right.

6. THE TOWER GARDEN IS GREAT FOR INDOOR GARDENING

The short growing season and the cool, short summers were the main reasons we got into Tower Garden gardening. We wanted to be able to grow more in a short summer, and also grow in the off season indoors all winter long. After trying to grow an indoor garden in soil, we knew we needed a better solution. Its no surprise that many commercial greenhouses grow plants hydroponically. It simply is better for indoor growing. The plants are always perfectly watered. Since there is no soil involved, it also limits the danger for bugs and mold.

7. Reasons to Grow a Tower Garden - grow your own salad greens.

My first look into the Tower Garden I had the impression that the garden was to expensive. I have since totally corrected my view. A high quality, locally grown, and pesticide free lettuce costs $4 in store. We eat one like that about every day. One Tower can grow 28 lettuces in a month. Do the math, 28 x $4 = $112.

A Tower Garden growing system, with extension, cage, and grow lights delivered to your door here in Canada comes to $102.64 a month for 12 months. You will still save about $10 dollars every month comparing to store bought lettuce. And after 12 months your lettuce is basically free. If you are in the US the numbers will be different.

AirGrown is a new aeroponics company that has developed the Airgown tower. The grow tower is a closed-loop system in a vertical stand. The vertical tower sits on a reservoir containing water and a plant nutrient solution which is misted on the plant's roots.

Thirty plant sites

The tower has dedicated "plant sites" allowing 30 separate plants to grow on a single vertical column. Since neither soil nor growing medium is used there is nothing for weeds to grow. Spraying with herbicides is not necessary and no toxic chemicals are left on the produce.

Vertical growing system

The inventor

Robert Scott Simmons from Indiantown of Florida is the inventor of Airgrow towers. The patent for the system was filed on September 11, 2009 and granted on July 24, 2012.

Mother helped me

After creating early models that worked, but about which his mother said he needed a better design, he eventually built the now patented aeroponics system. It includes a tower with conical tiers to house plants, a liquid nutrient reservoir, a pump to transport the nutrients and a power supply.

"Robert's mom said it was too ugly and tall originally, so I created a personal garden system specifically designed for her," he says. "She loves it and still plays with it every day."

The business

Simmons' residential aeroponics unit can hold 30 plants and a industrial version fits 60 per cubic yard. He's marketing the towers through his business, Airgrow.

"Aeroponics offers much better solutions for growing food—you get away from herbicides and you can use organic pesticides," he says. "We have to stop poisoning the Earth and ourselves. This opens the door for new science at a time when it's definitely needed. Aeroponics is how we're going to feed ourselves."

Followed NASA in aeroponics

Robert's AirGrown tower is a revolutionary vertical aeroponic plant growing system that provides economic benefits to the farming industry. Using aeroponic technology developed by NASA, the AirGrown system uses no growing medium and grows the root systems in a fine mist. With the AirGrown vertical aeroponic growing system plants can grow up to 45% faster than traditional farming methods.

Robert's plants yield cleaner, safer, tastier, and more aromatic produce. The AirGrown vertical tower is engineered to maximize food production in the smallest horizontal footprint and can be established in difficult or harsh environments where growing produce is hard or too expensive.

CONCLUSION

In order to prevent pests and diseases, it is recommended to clean the system after every harvest. Richard explains that "I designed it so that the aeroponic rings separate and fold up, so it is like stacking chairs." This user-friendliness also applies to the fog system; "if you experience clogged nozzles, you can disconnect the top, pull the whole thing out and drop another one in. As well as this, the towers can also be turned 360 degrees, for easy access for the crop workers and harvesting."

The cost for a grower to install such aeronopic tower installations depends entirely on the amount of extras they are interested in, and the unit's design was intended that it can built anywhere in the world. "If you go to our website, you will find a questionnaire, allowing you to make a wish list and receive all the information that you'll need," concludes Richard Gittings.